MEDIEVAL LIVES

Stonemason

ROBERT HULL

W
FRANKLIN WATTS
LONDON • SYDNEY

First published in 2008 by Franklin Watts

Franklin Watts
338 Euston Road
London NW1 3BH

Franklin Watts Australia
Level 17/207 Kent Street
Sydney, NSW 2000

A CIP catalogue record for this book is available
from the British Library.

Dewey number: 940.1

ISBN 978 0 7496 7741 1

Printed in China

Franklin Watts is a division of Hachette Children's
Books, an Hachette Livre UK company.

Artwork: Gillian Clements
Editor: Sarah Ridley
Editor in chief: John C. Miles
Designer: Simon Borrough
Art director: Jonathan Hair
Picture research: Diana Morris

Picture credits:
Ark Religion/Alamy: 23, 25b. Asperra Images/Alamy: 17t. Biblioteca Nazionale Marciana Venice / Gianni Dagli Orti /The Art Archive: front cover, 5. Biblioteca Nazionale Turin/Roger-Viollet /Bridgeman Art Library: 28. Bibliothèque de l'Arsenal Paris/Giraudon/Bridgeman Art Library: 36. Bibliothèque des Arts Decoratifs Paris/Archives Charmet/Bridgeman Art Library: 9. Bibliothèque Municipale Castres/Giraudon/Bridgeman Art Library: 12. Bibliothèque Nationale Paris/Alfredo Dagli Orti/The Art Archive: 20. Bibliothèque Nationale Paris/Giraudon/Bridgeman Art Library: 24, 33, 34. Bodleian Library Oxford/The Art Archive: 11. British Library Board/Bridgeman Art Library: 14. Alistair Campbell/UK City Images/Topfoto: 19. Castle Museum Ferrera/Alfredo Dagli Orti/The Art Archive: 26. Paul Felix Photography/Alamy: 21t. Michael Jenner/Alamy: 27. A F Kersting/AKG Images: 30. Paul Maegaert/Bridgeman Art Library: 35. MEPL/Alamy: 22. Florian Monheim/Roman von Götz/Alamy: 8. Musée Condé Chantilly/Giraudon/Bridgeman Art Library: 10, 16. Museo Opera del Duomo Firenze/Bridgeman Art Library: 32. James Osmond/Alamy: 39. Picturepoint/Topham: 13. Private Collection/Bridgeman Art Library: 40. Ray Roberts/Alamy: 41. St Lorenz Nuremburg/Bridgeman Art Library: 38. Jeff Saward/Labyrinthos Photo Library: 37. Spectrum Colour Library/HIP/Topfoto: 18. Staatsbibliothek Nuremburg/AKG Images: 31. Jack Sullivan/Alamy: 29b.
Every attempt has been made to clear copyright. Should there be any inadvertent omission please apply to the publisher for rectification.

CONTENTS

Introduction 8

Birth 10

Childhood and growing up 12

Training at the quarry 14

Training at the building site 16

Working as a rough-mason 18

Summoned to work at a castle 20

A real mason at the abbey 22

A growing reputation 24

Stone-carver 26

The lodge 28

Under-mason for the college 30

Master-mason for the cathedral 32

Designing the cathedral 34

Building the cathedral 36

Fulfilment and retirement 38

End of a life 40

Glossary/Websites/Timeline 42

Index 44

INTRODUCTION

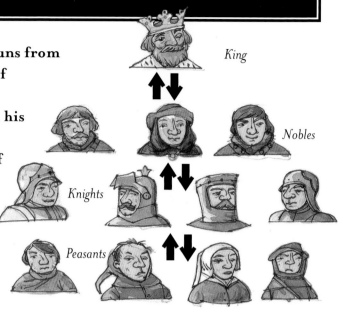

King

Nobles

Knights

Peasants

The 'medieval' period of European history runs from about 1000 to about 1500. It was a period of momentous events. In 1066 England was conquered by the Norman French king and his nobles; they and their descendants ruled it throughout medieval times. During most of the 14th century France and England fought the drawn-out Hundred Years War. Meanwhile, Christian crusaders fought with Muslim Arab armies over the control of Jerusalem. Then, in 1348, the Black Death killed around a third of the population of Europe – and of countries beyond.

'Feudal' society

At the beginning of this period European society was thoroughly 'feudal'. Kings owned all the land, but a class of knights was granted land in return for service in war. Knights made similar arrangements with holders of manorial estates, and they in turn with those below them, down to the peasants, who were granted a few acres of land, to which they were 'tied', in return for fees and heavy service obligations. This network of reciprocal agreements held society together.

As time went on, society became less feudally organised, as money payments and rents took the place of services and payments 'in kind'.

Gothic cathedrals such as this one were built throughout the Middle Ages.

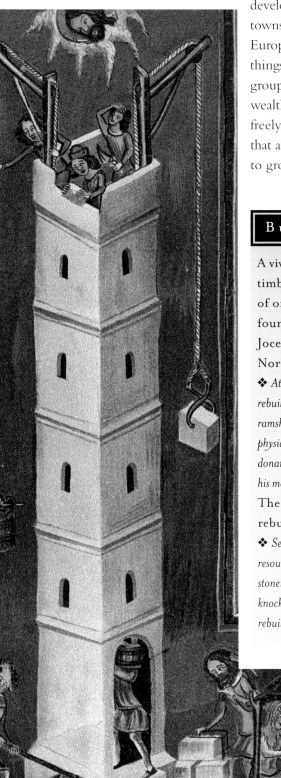

Medieval artists liked depicting mythical building sites; the Tower of Babel, shown here, was a popular subject.

As more transactions were made in money, more money came into circulation. There was a rapid development of trade and of towns, and the population of Europe grew. The ability to buy things with money spread to all groups, except the poorest. The wealthiest people in society spent freely on buildings in stone, a trend that accelerated when timber began to grow scarce and expensive.

Building in stone

A vivid picture of the shift from timber building to stone — and of one way it was funded — is found in the Chronicle of Jocelin, Abbot of Brakelond in Norfolk from 1173:

❖ *At this time too, our almonry was rebuilt in stone — formerly it had been ramshackle and of wood. Walter the physician, then almoner, gave a large donation of money that he had made from his medical practice.* ❖

The guest-house was also rebuilt:

❖ *See how on the abbot's orders the court resounds to the sound of pickaxes and stonemasons' tools as the guest-house is knocked down… May God provide for the rebuilding.* ❖

Churches abound

The French chronicler Ralph Glaber, writing in the 11th century, had this to say about the boom in church-building:

❖ *It is as though the very world had shaken herself and cast off her old age, to clothe herself everywhere in a white robe of churches.* ❖

Building explosion

The early medieval period in particular — from about 1000 to 1250 — was an astonishing time for building, especially ecclesiastical buildings in stone. Cathedrals, abbeys, nunneries and monasteries built of stone, with numerous outbuildings, sprang up in or near large towns, or in the countryside; stone churches replaced timber buildings in thousands of villages. It is calculated that in France there was a church for every 200 inhabitants.

It was not only the Church that built and built. Kings did too, and some noblemen. Numerous castles and colleges and even manor-houses of stone appeared, each one needing an army of stonemasons to quarry stone, cut and carve it, lift and lay it in place.

Many of these stone buildings, some glorious, some modest and plain, survive today. This book will follow the typical life story of one of the stonemasons who worked on these buildings.

BIRTH

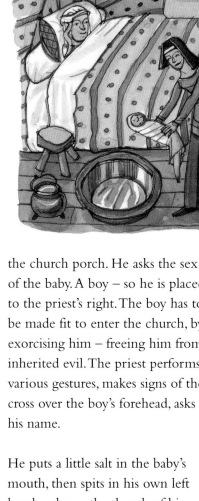

In an upstairs room in a fairly large house in the town, the stonemason's wife is about to give birth. A midwife of the town is present, and two women neighbours. No men are to enter the room.

To help make sure of a safe and easy delivery, the mason's wife has asked for a scroll to be laid across her belly during childbirth, with a cross on it one 15th the size of the cross on which Jesus was crucified. As her time draws close, the women all pray to the saints, and urge the mother to do so as well. The child – a boy – is born safely (right). The charm, and the prayers, seem to have worked.

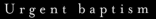

Urgent baptism

A 14th-century poem by Robert Mannyng grimly stresses the urgency of early baptism.

❖ *Adam's sin was so severe*
That there is none to God so dear
Who will not to Hell be gone
Unless he is washed in the font of stone. ❖

Baptism

The parents want the boy baptised as soon as the godparents – two godfathers and a godmother – can come to the church and give him a name.

Carrying his Latin Manual, or book of services, the priest meets midwife, baby and godparents in the church porch. He asks the sex of the baby. A boy – so he is placed to the priest's right. The boy has to be made fit to enter the church, by exorcising him – freeing him from inherited evil. The priest performs various gestures, makes signs of the cross over the boy's forehead, asks his name.

He puts a little salt in the baby's mouth, then spits in his own left hand and uses the thumb of his right to moisten the boy's ears and nostrils with saliva – the way Christ healed a deaf mute. Two or three more signings of the cross, and the party go into the church, to the font.

A baby being baptised at the stone font.

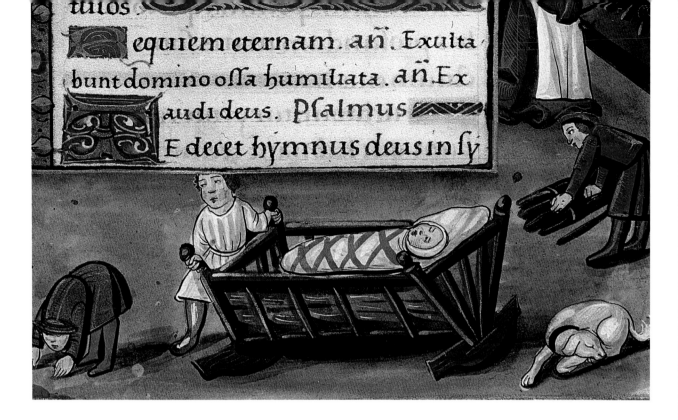

equiem eternam. an. Exulta
bunt domino ossa humiliata. an. Ex
audi deus. Psalmus
E decet hymnus deus in sy

Three full immersions take place in the water of the font. Then the baby is wrapped in a blessed robe, the godparents are told to teach the child simple prayers, and the parents (though the mother is not present) to keep him safe.

The mason gives a small feast for family, neighbours, friends and godparents in the evening. They bring the baby boy gifts – a small toy or a little money.

The 'churching'

The mother cannot go to church to give thanks for having safely given birth. She is not allowed to touch a holy object or enter a holy place for 40 days because, having given birth, she is considered 'unclean'. Only when she is 'churched', purified in a ceremony at the church, where she goes with women neighbours and friends, can she resume normal life.

Though the mason and his wife are, like most people, Christians, they put food by the baby's cradle at night, to appease any wicked spirit or witch who might want to harm their child.

The little boy is soon crawling, then walking, at first with the help of a wooden frame his father made, then on his own. He has to be watched carefully, in case he wanders near the fire, or bowls of boiling water, or out of doors into the street, which is full of horse-drawn carts, cattle coming and going, roaming dogs, and pigs sometimes, escaped from pens. He survives these dangers, and is growing up strong and healthy.

A baby wrapped in swaddling bands in its cradle, which is on rockers, being rocked by an older child.

Exorcising sin

The Christian Church believed that every baby inherited humankind's 'original sin', committed by Adam and Eve and handed on ever since. This sin needed to be got rid of, exorcised, by the baby renouncing sin in the baptism service. The priest asked the baby simple questions – in Latin. The godparents replied on his behalf.
❖ *Abrenuncias Sathane? (Do you renounce Satan?)*
Abrenuncio. (I renounce him.)
Quid petis? (What do you seek?)
Baptismum. (Baptism.) ❖
After that, all is well.

CHILDHOOD AND GROWING UP

Even the healthiest little children have illnesses. When he is four, the stonemason's son falls sick, as do many children in the town. His mother is desperately worried. She measures the length of his small body and has her husband buy a candle of exactly the same length, to take to the church as an offering. He recovers – the cures have worked.

Home schooling

At the age of five the boy's mother starts to teach him his letters. She buys biscuits, sugary fruit and cakes in the shape of letters. His father gives him a primer, with the alphabet in, and buys educational toys, like the little windowed box which shows one letter at a time as a little wheel turns round the scroll inside. He also carves small stone animals for his son and buys metal soldiers and a mechanical bird with a moveable tongue.

School

The parents want their son to learn, because the father is keen for him to become a stonemason, perhaps a master, who might one day build a cathedral. At seven he goes to a school in the church, where a priest teaches reading and writing, Latin grammar and arithmetic. The boy will need to know Latin to read the many documents and papers of the time.

Boys being taught to read by a priest.

Parents whose children fell ill were at the mercy of travelling quacks with 'remedies' that never worked, except to get money from people. One fraud was to call at a house pretending to be a doctor from abroad, and his interpreter. The doctor examines the child, who might be perfectly healthy, muttering nonsense words. The mother asks the interpreter what the 'doctor' says. He says the child is sick, but luckily he has a cure, some powder wrapped in a bit of paper – for which the mother pays several shillings. Other 'remedies' were more drastic, like letting blood from behind the ears to cure dizziness.

Childhood games

When he is not at school, there are games to play in the street: spinning a top, running along on a stick-horse, playing with little windmills on sticks, rolling stones. There are fairs to go to, feast-days to have holidays on.

By the time he is nine or ten, the boy occasionally goes with his father to work, at the quarry or the building site. He watches stones being hewed and shaped and carried, and mortar being mixed. At the site his father even gives him a chisel and hammer to carve a piece of spoiled stone.

·Confabulator·

Confabulato. iñ. é. uña cir fompni. Electo ⁊ uciens ñe uolctis dormir. uuiam. delectrib; iñ meliorati et digouier ⁊ fenf ⁊ ſp̃. floeiunium audur plcs ⁊ fabulatores. cu uoluit ñ unū auo Remō nocti iponcir ſolennui. illi q̃ audur nō cuſp. Conucir oib; ⁊plonib; oib; etatib;. pter puis. oi tp̃; ſi mag̃ breme ⁊ regioi bitate.

Children and parents gathered round the fire.

Drawing like a mason

He gives him simple drawings to do, using a pair of compasses and a square of the kind that he uses when planning a piece of building. The young boy plays with circles, half-circles, intersecting circles, circles in squares, straight lines ending in arcs – the basic shapes buildings are designed with. He feels he is working like a real mason. At 13 he has already decided to be a stonemason and work alongside his father.

TRAINING AT THE QUARRY

The teenage boy begins work with his father, who is master-mason for a new church a few miles from their home town. The boy will go round and help where he can, learning as he goes. At 15, he is old enough – and strong enough – to do some work as his father's assistant and be trained by him.

Travel expenses

Masons would usually be paid for time spent travelling between building site and quarry, or to look for a suitable quarry. The Westminster Fabric Roll, a kind of account book detailing costs of materials for the building ('fabric'), lists a mason's travelling expenses:

❖ *6d per day for 8 days for riding to the quarries to choose and examine good stones.* ❖

Health and safety

His first 'schoolroom' is the quarry. The mason warns his son about the dangers of quarries and building sites, and reminds him to keep his wits about him. Stones, wood, heavy tools – and men sometimes – fall from scaffolding; platforms collapse; blocks of stone fall off carts. The previous week a mason's legs were broken by a fully loaded cart.

Masons rough-dressing blocks of stone, while woodmen cut down trees.

Though there were attempts to regulate them, wages on building sites were probably fixed informally, as soon as the master or under-master was in a position to judge the mason's level of skill. So at Caernarvon Castle in October 1304, there were 53 masons receiving 17 different rates of pay. In October 1316, there were 24 masons on 12 different wage-rates. The presence of 'servants' and young men, or apprentices, at different stages in their training, may have contributed to this variety of pay-scales, as might the presence of some women labourers.

Learning his trade

The son learns from his father about building stone. Stone suitable for castles, town walls or pavements is usually not right for shaping or intricate carving. That is why this quarry has been chosen, ten miles from the church, even though the hills between the quarry and the church will add to the cost of transport. Transport usually puts up the price of quarried stone by about four times anyway, unless it can be taken by water some of the way, which it can here. It also keeps weight and cartage costs down to carve some stones before they leave the quarry. Sometimes cities plunder their own walls to build cheaper churches.

His father takes him to see a skilled quarryman at work at a new rock face, estimating how wide the layer of stone is and where best to start cutting. He uses a pickaxe and crowbar, and wooden wedges. He makes the back-breaking work look straightforward.

Stone dust is everywhere in the air. The boy watches labourers with a crane and claw lifting stones into wheelbarrows – a recent invention – and carrying them to waiting carts.

The mason's mark

His father gives the boy his mark, the mark he will put on every stone he cuts. A master-mason has to know who carved every stone even in a huge cathedral. Any stone the wrong size or shape, or out of line, or hollowed instead of flat, will result in the mason responsible losing pay.

The boy's main training work now is to 'scapple' hewn stones, which means shaping them very roughly, 'rough-dressing' them with an axe and a hammer, ready for carting down to the river and on to the building site.

The son helps his father with some of the rough work at the quarry.

TRAINING AT THE BUILDING SITE

As master-mason, the boy's father can make sure his son experiences all the different tasks on the building site (below), so that he will begin to understand the work of masons.

With several labourers, the boy carries water, lime and sand to the man mixing mortar. He watches him at work, then carries the mortar in a tub on his back –

urgently, in case it starts to set – into the church and across to the screen being built up with beautifully carved stones.

Later he helps the 'setters' to put intricate mouldings and tracery into windows and arches. He helps the men building the tower to lay stone blocks in place, sometimes high up on the scaffolding.

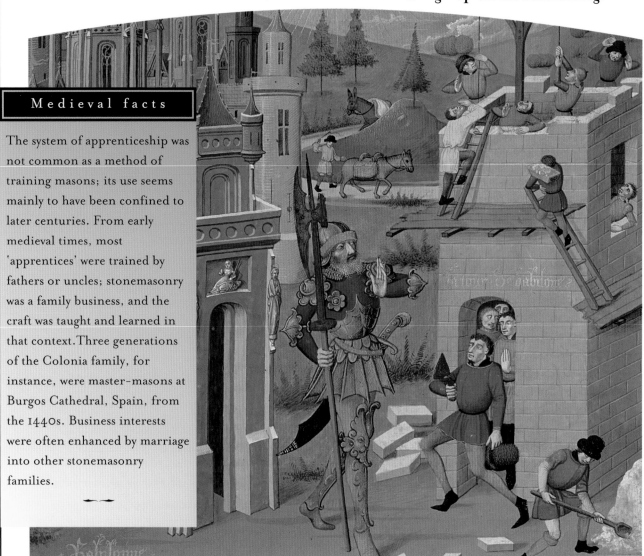

Medieval facts

The system of apprenticeship was not common as a method of training masons; its use seems mainly to have been confined to later centuries. From early medieval times, most 'apprentices' were trained by fathers or uncles; stonemasonry was a family business, and the craft was taught and learned in that context. Three generations of the Colonia family, for instance, were master-masons at Burgos Cathedral, Spain, from the 1440s. Business interests were often enhanced by marriage into other stonemasonry families.

Dressing stone

Then his father sets him to work as a 'cutter', shaping rough-dressed blocks to the exact sizes they're needed, keeping the edges straight, the curves correctly curved, the corners right-angled, and the surfaces flat. It's difficult to get them all right. Then, after months of dressing all kinds of stones, destined for different parts of the church, he is given drawings of one or two small detailed shapes to carve on bits of spare stone: an oak-leaf and an ox. This is even more difficult, but the boy finds the work fascinating.

His training is going well. He learns quickly how to use the set-square and compasses. He learns to use a variety of other tools, including a range of chisels, to create smooth surfaces, and a large cone-shaped mallet of apple-wood for very delicate work. For months he works on decorating blocks with mouldings – designs carved onto the stone with the help of a 'template', a thin layer of wood which has the exact shape needed.

To the tracing-floor

The father is very pleased with his son's progress. Now he takes the son to the workshop where he transfers his own scale drawings on parchment, enlarged to life-size, onto a 'tracing-floor' of plaster, which is brushed clean for each drawing, leaving ghostly outlines underneath as examples for the stone to be carved on. One or two life-size designs are even engraved on the stone floor of the church, ready for copying.

His son watches, then he settles to practise the same skills with two or three designs his father needs for window openings high in the church. He also works on designs from the buildings he has made drawings of. Then he spends many months on the freehand carving of things he has observed or drawn – oak leaves, an apple, a gate, piglets and human faces.

The father watches his son develop over several years (right). His son seems skilful enough to do well as a stonemason.

A mason's mark chiselled on a stone block.

WORKING AS A ROUGH-MASON

The young man is ready to set out on his own. If it weren't for the fact that his father, who has become prosperous, wants to spend more time on the other trades he and his wife have begun to build up, the young man would have remained working with him. Now his father prefers to run an inn and tend grazing animals. But also, his lungs have been affected by inhaling stone dust over so many years.

On his own

All this does not deter the young man from his chosen vocation, and he hears that masons are needed for repair work on a damaged bridge in the nearby town. The upkeep of the bridge is the working responsibility of the wardens of the bridge, but the funds for it come from all the surrounding towns and villages whose travellers and traders use it. One group of villages look after a pier and a cutwater, another group pay for the upkeep of the roadway.

He presents himself to the master-mason in charge of the bridge works, and tells him what he has learned over the last few years, from cutting and carrying stone, to carving in freestone from templates and drawing up designs.

He is taken on as a rough-mason, at not much above the labourer's rate, to be paid by the hour. He has to rough-dress blocks of stone,

ready for the skilled 'cutters' to shape up exactly – work he knows he can do just as well. He must cut into the stone both his own mason's mark and the sign for where it will go on the bridge. He is warned that every block is checked by the master-mason, and any faults will mean loss of up to two days' pay.

This medieval stone bridge at Cahors, in central France, still stands.

This mural tower in Canterbury would have been built by masons working for the town. The clock is modern.

that he has more work to do in the town, constructing a short tunnel, and building walls of stone – as firebreaks – between thatched timber houses: would the young man like to join him on those projects?

'Yes' is the answer. After working on both projects, the young mason gains more experience and a growing reputation for being hard-working and trustworthy. He is picking up more of the geometry of construction and feels that his mason's career is now properly launched.

Perhaps he can afford to marry the young woman worker he met on the first building site. His father promises him that when he marries he will give him a small house in the town.

First success

His first work goes well. The master-mason is pleased with him and gives him the work he wants, which is to dress stones exactly, to make them ready for laying in place. The master-mason even trusts him to go to the quarry to choose more stone. When the bridge repairs are finished, he says

SUMMONED TO WORK AT A CASTLE

The young man's first work away from home is 80 kilometres away. He has been 'impressed' – summoned – by the King, to work on the stonework of the main hall in one of his new castles. It takes him over two days to walk there, carrying his compasses and set-square. The other tools, hammers and chisels, as well as protective gloves, are to be provided by his employer.

The working day

The under-mason explains that his working day will be from sunrise – before 5 am in summer – to sunset for five-and-a-half days a week, finishing at noon on the Saturday. He has one hour for dinner, 30 minutes for 'sleeping' and 30 minutes for 'drinking' in the afternoon. He will be paid for feast-days and days of travel, though not when bad weather stops work. If his work is not up to standard, 'uncunning', he can be dismissed. That would be done before noon. The work will last for several weeks.

Because he is still inexperienced, he is to work again as a rough-mason, at 4d a day, summer rate, rough-dressing stones. With all his father's training, and some experience, he feels he will be accepted everywhere soon as a real mason, but he has to prove himself again here. The stones he rough-dresses must be right. Otherwise he will not only lose pay; he will lose the under-mason's confidence. Once he gains it, though, he might be given stone to finish properly, and perhaps even carve designs.

Labourers and masons at work on a castle, with an overseer on his horse.

Poor time-keeping

A 1495 statute regulating labour in England laid down winter and summer working hours – before 5 am to 7 or 8 pm in summer, 'from daylight till dark' in winter. The preamble to the act suggests that the hours were often not well observed; it reveals that:

❖ *... a number of workmen and labourers ... waste a large part of the day, coming late to work, and leaving early, lingering over breakfast and dinner, and sleeping overlong after noon.* ❖

A collection of the stonemason's many tools, with some templates.

Impressment by the monarch might even threaten to take masons from their work on large and important projects. In 1441 All Souls College in Oxford had to obtain a royal order exempting men working there from being impressed to work on Eton College.

The stonemason with his basket of tools.

To work

He gets his tools – chisels, hammer, stone-axe, wooden mallet – from the store in the lodge, the shed-like structure built against the walls. Here he will do some of his work and have his midday rest – until the bell clangs to start work. His living- and sleeping-quarters are in a hostel that the employers have built nearby.

It is the young man's first experience of a large building site. The ceaseless din of it all takes him aback at first. From early morning until nightfall the air rings with the squeal of pulleys and windlasses, the noises of hammers, chisels, saws and axes; and with voices shouting orders and warnings. It sounds chaotic, but it is not; the site is highly organised.

The under-mason soon sees the quality of his work. He gives him more responsibility. The kind of blocks that he has been rough-dressing he now dresses to precise sizes and shapes. The under-mason promotes his assistant to the rank of mason proper, and increases his wage from 4d to 6d a day.

The mason and the young woman decide to marry. In a year or so his father will give him the small house he promised.

A REAL MASON AT THE ABBEY

The young man has earned the right to be called a 'mason'. That is a beginning, but, his father says, there are many ranks of mason on most big building sites, and it will take time and hard work to become one of the better-paid, and even longer to fulfil his dream to become a master-mason and design a cathedral.

That is the future. His next step now, he believes, must be to work on a large church somewhere. There is a new abbey church to be built 30 kilometres from his home, which is still his parents' house when he is not away working. He will walk home to see his wife whenever he can.

A mason cuts a piece of stone to size with a frame saw.

To the abbey church

With compass and square, he sets off for the abbey. Once there, he heads for the lodge, a long, one-storeyed wooden structure built against a wall of the small old church that was badly damaged in a storm, and is now being demolished to make space for the grander building that will replace it – the abbey church.

In the lodge there is a space for laying out and tracing drawings, and a work area for making the wooden templates that are aids to producing exact repeats of carved work. Tools are also stored and sharpened here, and repaired; and stones are cut, dressed and carved. It is in the lodge that the master-mason is often to be found, at work himself, or discussing work with other masons, or hiring labour.

First skilled carving

The young mason tells him about his work, his training and experience. The master-mason takes him on as a journeyman mason, paid by the day, and gives him work to do dressing stones. He is soon convinced by the young mason's abilities, and asks him to do a trial carving of a mouse on one face of some spoiled stone. The young man tackles this with enthusiasm; it is his first chance since his training to show how well he can carve 'freestone' – stone which can easily be shaped on all its faces and sculpted into patterns or life-like representations of foliage, animals, human faces and so on.

He carves the mouse to the master's satisfaction, and is given the task of first dressing the curved stones of a doorway arch and then carving into them the chevron shapes that will give their pleasing patterned effect to the archway.

In time he is asked to try other shapes too. He enjoys sculpting grotesque faces like those he's seen on other buildings. One that he completes, of a man with toothache, becomes one of the abbey church's gargoyles. He knows his new son will like it when he's old enough.

Tools

In some places at least, the tools masons carried with them were bought by their employers, and so in effect provided by them. This item appears in the fabric roll at Vale Royal Abbey in 1278:

❖ *Paid to (11 named) masons, carrying their tools with them, to wit, 20 hatchets, and 48 irons for carving stones, 10s, because it is the custom that their tools, if they bring any, shall be bought.* ❖

Medieval facts

The word 'sculptor' seems to have been seldom used in medieval times, except in Italy. There were artist-craftsmen all over Europe doing work that we would call 'sculpture' – wonderful sculpture (right) too – but who were thought of as 'cutters' or 'carvers' of stone, albeit highly-skilled and experienced ones, rather than masons in a special category. Nonetheless, the reputations of the most skilled cutters and carvers travelled far, which is perhaps why sometimes, experienced as they were in all kinds of stonemasonry, they readily became under-masons or master-masons.

A GROWING REPUTATION

T**he young mason spends two years dressing stone and carving designs on the abbey church. In winter, when building stops because of the frosts, he continues to work on his carving and on drawing geometrical designs.**

Work stops

The flow of money and bequests has temporarily dried up. The main cause is the war that the King has embarked on. The abbey has to sell precious objects and divert spare funds into paying taxes to finance this war. He has more opportunities now to walk the 20 miles home to his wife and son in their small new house.

In the meantime, by different routes, from rumour to recommendation, the young mason's skill and capacity for hard work, and his artistic talent with hammer, chisel and mallet become known to other potential employers. With two other masons, he is rewarded by being presented – a considerable honour – with gifts of winter clothing.

The image-carver

When work starts again, he is asked one day by the bishop, as he

A working drawing for part of the great cathedral in Laon, France, showing the ox-heads that decorate the pinnacles.

tours the new building with the master-mason, if he will work as an 'imaginator', or image-maker, in one large and two smaller churches being built or rebuilt in his diocese. He will be able to

In 1414 the authorities of Valencia Cathedral, engaged on preparations for a new bell tower, had a contract drawn up paying their 'architect' for researching bell tower structures far afield.

❖ *It is settled that Pedro Balaquer, an 'able architect', shall receive 50 florins from the fabric fund of the new campanile (bell tower) ... in payment of expenses on the journey he made to Laredo, Narbonne and other cities, in order to see them and examine their towers and campaniles, so as to discover from them the most elegant and suitable form for the Cathedral of Valencia.* ❖

carve some delicate stonework. As imaginator, he will lead three or four other sculptors, and so be able to choose what he will work on, and how to treat it.

The young mason wonders if his ambition to be a master-builder will be helped or held back by working, perhaps for several years, as a carver of images. In the end he decides that if he builds up a reputation as a mason who can execute the highest quality images and construct memorable and moving designs, while leading others, it must help him rise further in his craft.

Finding inspiration

Before he begins to carve a single piece, though, the bishop wishes him to travel to several other churches and cathedrals he knows, one or two in another country, to see what kinds of decorative work are done there, and collect ideas. He wants the young man to pick up ideas and take inspiration from the work of the best artists in stone. The bishop wants his churches to have the most up-to-date and interesting images possible.

On his travels the young mason sees sculptures he had never encountered or imagined: such as the oxen sculpted on high pinnacles, in honour of the animals who draw carts. He makes sketch after sketch, and by the time he returns, his drawing-book and his mind are both full of ideas.

This statue of the Virgin and Child is in Reims, France.

'Rewards', usually in money or clothing, were sometimes paid to masons for good work. In the Eton College accounts there is this entry from 1445-46:

❖ *In various rewards made to setters of stone... for their diligent labour in hot weather... Henry Roo 12s... and to five ... setters of freestone, 5s 8s, 6s 4d, 2s 8d, 3s 4d, 3s 4d; but then to a 'carver' 20s.* ❖

STONE-CARVER

The master-mason tells the stone-carvers about the kind of images the bishop hopes to see in his churches. He would like figures from a religious story over each west door; somewhere in each nave he wants a strong image of the church's patron saint; but he leaves their imaginations free to work on things like capitals, gargoyles and panels.

Our carver visits the churches, all three within miles of each other. He decides to work first on two capitals for a nave, the space where the village people gather. He will carve the capitals on site, in the large church's lodge.

Gathering ideas

He discusses with the other carvers what they will do. In their lodge at the largest church, they spend time drawing sketches for possible designs. They exchange ideas and compare drawings. The carver's own notebook reminds him of vivid images he has seen: a tombstone with a panel showing scholars listening intently to a lecture; another with a full-size sculpture of a woman, lying down reading a book; a grim façade depicting the torments of Hell; some relief carvings of a Bible story. And many more, including some hideous devils.

He decides first on a homely, slightly comic scene with a hint of sin in it – a boy stealing fruit from an orchard. It will please the ordinary worshippers, as well as –

he hopes – the master-mason, and perhaps amuse their patron. As he starts carving, another idea comes to him too. When he gets time he will draw it.

This 12th-century carving of a boy picking fruit is in the cathedral in Ferrara, Italy.

Medieval facts

Some of the finest carvings in medieval churches and cathedrals were done in pure white marble, some in the polished Purbeck or Corfe marble which was really a compressed limestone. Many, from the 15th century on, were done in polished white alabaster. Chellaston in Derbyshire was known for its high-grade alabaster. In 1414 Alexander de Berneville, a master-mason working for the Abbey of Fécamp, France, travelled there to buy some, paying 40 gold crowns for it to be shipped to France through Hull.

Carving images

Work gets underway at the large church. The carver's first capital is eventually ready. He marks it with his own mark, and a number indicating where it will be placed. He likes it, as does the master. The painter will give colour to the face on the capital, so it will gaze down into the nave even more intently.

He starts work on his second, more complicated idea; it is St Matthew writing, receiving inspiration from an angel who bends down to him. Before he notices, one of the sculptors nearly spoils his angel; carving the foot, he gives it a sandal. Of the main religious figures, only the Virgin Mary, a human being, has shoes – not God, or Jesus, or angels. It is luckily not too late. The carver is skilled enough to chisel away the sandal, down to the bare foot hiding in the stone, before anyone notices. This too proves successful.

His work is approved of, and the master gives him a new panel to work on, to fill with a design of his own. He decides on a favourite story, the creation of the animals.

An effigy of a noble and his wife rest on their tomb in Spilsby, Lincolnshire. Nobles liked to be commemorated by sculptures such as these.

THE LODGE

The skilled stone-carver has spent much of his time in the lodge at the largest church, working alongside other masons. In various ways, he has learned to appreciate the lodge. It gives him shelter from bad weather. He can take blunt or damaged chisels and axes along to the smith to have them sharpened or repaired on the spot. He finds, too, that as trust builds up between different masons, ideas are shared more and more; notebooks and drawings are lent, know-how exchanged. The lodge becomes as much a living community as a building of wood.

Sharing experiences

One of the most helpful things is to hear stories of the others' travels to buildings elsewhere in the country, and in other countries. It thrills him to learn about wonderful buildings, amazing high spires, even a spire that is not solid but a frame of stone you can see through. He hears tell of buttresses that 'fly' to walls, of statues on the skyline summits of the highest pinnacles of the roof.

He hears about towers that fall because they were built too high, on columns that were not solid enough; about walls that lean and crack and bulge, because the foundations were shallow or filled with the wrong material, or because the mortar was not mixed properly.

The emperor Charlemagne founds the abbey at Aix-la-Chapelle in this manuscript illustration, which clearly shows masons at work and cranes lifting blocks of stone.

Code of conduct

Two of the other carvers know of attempts to get all masons in the country to agree on rules for their craft and have them written down. Rules such as that training, or being an apprentice, should last for at least five years – some say seven; that no mason should take another's work; that masons should take communion once a year; that they should not give away to non-masons the secrets of their trade – such as how to construct designs from geometric shapes.

These are things a good mason practises anyway, the carver believes, but it would be good to have them written down and agreed on, perhaps all over the country. It would show patrons that masons take their work seriously, and consider being a mason an honour. Masons are not of high social standing, they work with their hands. But the skilled carving mason is an artist, the master-mason is a leader, engineer and a designer, who works with set-square and compasses to contrive designs for great buildings. Their work needs more recognition and status.

Members of the lodge, with tools and symbols of the craft.

Symbols and masons' tools decorate this stained-glass window of a modern Freemason's lodge.

UNDER-MASON FOR THE COLLEGE

The mason soon takes another step upwards. His highly-skilled work as a carver of images has often been praised by the bishop. He is asked to take on the job of under-mason, sometimes called 'warden' or 'parleur', in the building of a college. He will be the person to explain the master-mason's ideas, and make sure that masons understand the plans. He also has to keep a watchful eye on building materials, tools and equipment, which can mysteriously go missing.

The under-mason

As deputy to the master-mason, he will help him appoint new masons. He will have responsibility for some of the designs and drawings that will be needed. So not only will he visit the quarry and be on hand all over the building site, he will spend a good deal of time in the lodge workshop checking on the work of other masons, and some time working out designs and doing drawings on parchment and designs on the 'tracing-floor'.

Meanwhile, masons come to the site looking for work. He asks them to do trial work on spoiled stones in the workshop, or put to one side outside the lodge. He checks to see what tools they have brought with them. The building works usually supply and repair the cheaper tools, like axes, hatchets, hammers and chisels, but masons are expected to bring their own set-square and compasses with them, simply because they are too expensive to provide in numbers.

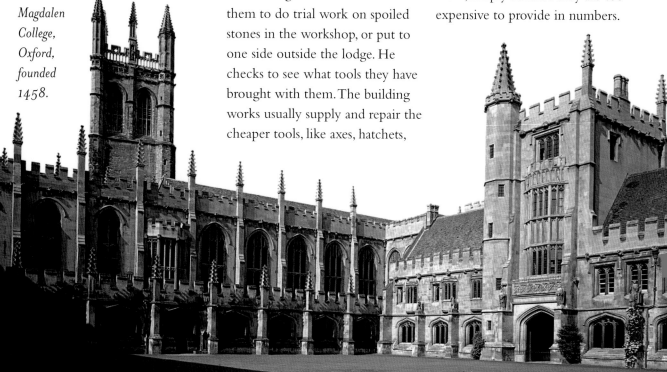

Magdalen College, Oxford, founded 1458.

This 15th-century German painting shows a skilled roofer at work in Nuremburg.

Medieval facts

The under-master or warden probably played a major role in looking after the lodge's tools. On a large site there were a great number. An inventory of tools and implements in the York Minster Fabric Rolls for 1399 lists, amongst other things:
69 stone-axes,
a big gavel,
24 mallets,
1 compass,
2 tracing boards,
1 samm hatchet,
1 handsaw,
1 shovel,
1 wheelbarrow,
2 buckets,
1 large cart with wheels and
2 smaller carts.
Other heavy tools for laying stones were kept in the crypt, including stone-hammers and windlasses. These were almost certainly not the possessions of the masons themselves. Not mentioned are plumb-lines, squares, levels and other compasses, which probably were their own. Other apparatus for laying stones was kept in the crypt. All this was probably owned by the Chapter.

Site manager

With the master-carpenter, he supervises the building of a second lodge for the works. The old lodge provides working space for about 20 masons, but more masons are being taken on as the college grows, and more tools are being bought and need to be stored. There are a few training or apprentice masons, too, working with older masons, mainly family members, and space has to be found for them.

Since the college is out in the country, 50 kilometres or so from his home, the under-mason also has to make sure that workers are accommodated properly in the hostel – a simple wood structure – specially constructed for them.

These responsibilities are time-consuming, and take him away from his beloved stone, mallet and chisels, but he knows he is learning fast about the complicated organisation of a building site.

MASTER-MASON FOR THE CATHEDRAL

A hundred and more miles away, a new cathedral is to be built. Four well-known masons have been asked to travel there, to meet the money-providing patron – the bishop himself – and the Chapter, and describe what their plans would be if appointed to the position of master-mason.

The skilled mason-carver and 'imaginator', with fresh experience as an under-mason, is one of those summoned. He has thought long and often about the cathedral he would like to build, and has a hundred drawings of his ideas in his notebook, which of course he takes with him, along with one or two models in wood.

To the interview

The mason makes the long journey on foot. The bishop and Chapter give him some idea of what they want. An important consideration is size. The city is growing fast; its population is increasing. The cathedral must be high enough, long enough and impressive enough – both beautiful and modern in spirit – to be worthy of a great city, and of course to hold a large number of people.

This model of the cupola atop the Duomo in Florence was the work of its brilliant architect, Filippo Brunelleschi (1377-1446).

The mason shows them drawings and plans. He sets down the model he's brought with him, and explains clearly what he would do. The patron understands the model better than the complicated drawings. He and the Chapter like both the model and the mason's clear, dynamic way of talking. They appoint him. His young wife is thrilled, even though it means they will have to move house.

Head-hunted

The reputation of a fine stone-carver might spread from country to country, so that a commission could come from far afield. In 1287 the provost of Paris registered an agreement for a stone-cutter to go to Sweden to work as a master:

❖ *Etienne de Bonneuil came before us, agreeing to be master-builder of the church of Uppsala in Sweden... He agreed that he would take with him... such companions and apprentices as he shall see fit.* ❖

Appointed as master-mason

The master is told he will direct a large number of craftsmen – carpenters and joiners constructing pulpits and choirs, pews and screen; blacksmiths making hinges, locks, nails and railings; glaziers producing windows and coloured images; plumbers putting down lead sheeting on the roof; painters painting wall-scenes and images.

Many of the craftsmen he will meet and select himself, but he will have an under-master or warden to help him, and a clerk of the works to handle all the business details, including wages. His own wage, he finds, is to be

Another view of the construction of the cathedral at Aix-la-Chapelle (see page 28).

about four times what he earned as an image-carver, and he will be allowed to claim travel expenses.

The bishop and Chapter are pleased that he is more than

willing to take on all this responsibility. Before they meet again, he is asked to prepare even more designs and drawings, so that they understand even better what he will be aiming to do.

33

DESIGNING THE CATHEDRAL

The site of the new cathedral has been chosen by the bishop and his Chapter, the money for making a beginning of it provided by the bishop himself. Work will begin at the east end, the most sacred space, where the high altar will be, and the relics kept. The cathedral is designed so that the east window will light up at sunrise on the birthday of the cathedral saint. As soon as possible this east end will be roofed, and consecrated, so that pilgrims can come.

Completing the plans

These things are decided before the master-mason starts work there. Now he needs to complete his plans for the cathedral. He translates his sketches into detailed scale drawings: of nave and arches; of chancel, altar and side-chapels; then of the higher levels, triforium and clerestory, vaulted roof and spire, which he wants to be the highest for hundreds of miles.

He is ambitious to design a beautiful cathedral, which will have higher and wider pointed arches than other cathedrals he has seen, and less heavy stonework, so there will be more glass and light. He travels to other cathedrals and building sites to see how other masters have solved these problems.

This plan of the tower of Laon Cathedral also shows a bearded head and a Gothic window.

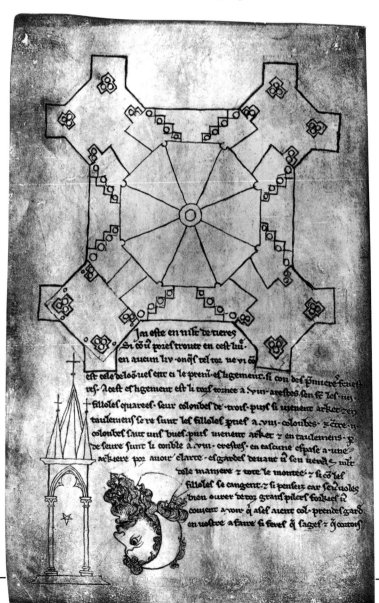

34

The cloister, or covered quadrangle walk, of Gloucester Cathedral (built 1370-1410), boasts a fan-vaulted ceiling.

Too many walls and spires and towers fall down for him to take any chances with his design. A high tower or spire always sets up a great stress on the columns beneath, round the crossing, in the middle of the building. And the high pointed vaults he wants to build also set up stresses, trying to push the walls outward, where they come down onto the columns. He studies one cathedral where the walls are braced against this outward push by the kind of 'flying' buttresses he's heard about, built not against the wall as part of it, but standing separately.

Lime-pits and quarry

He also has to make sure that lime-pits — for making lime mortar — are dug months in advance of the start of building, and perhaps more important, decide which of three nearby quarries to use. With the bishop, he visits all three, and decides he would like to use the furthest away of the three. The extra few miles will increase carting expenses, but it has just the kind of honey-coloured sandstone he wants for 'his' cathedral. The bishop agrees. Not all the stone will come from there — not the marble he will need for some things, or the alabaster for intricate carving.

He is now ready to set in motion the actual building of the cathedral.

BUILDING THE CATHEDRAL

The master's first task is to supervise the pegging out on the ground, with ropes, of the dimensions of the cathedral. The blacksmith makes him a square-sectioned length of iron, about 16 feet (4.8 metres) long. This 'pole' will measure out all the cathedral's main dimensions, vertical and horizontal.

So, down the length of the cathedral, the distance between one column and the next is one pole, as is the distance between each column and the outer walls, so the side-aisles are a pole wide, while the nave is two, making the whole structure four poles wide. The length from east to west will be twelve poles. Its height will be a breathtaking six poles.

Final preparations

Next, the master has the foundations dug and filled with rubble to make them solid. The foundations have to be deep enough. When they are shallow – or when the infill isn't sturdy enough – sinking occurs, or cracking; walls can lean and even collapse.

The master-mason and his patron check on the progress of building works, inspecting the work of masons, carpenters and mortarers.

Medieval facts

In laying out the design for a cathedral, the basis of measurement seemed to be a large unit of length or module – a length which might vary from country to country and even region to region, but not within the site; it was the fact that all spaces and lengths were planned and measured out in terms of the modular length that helped give buildings their proportionality and balance.

In England the 'rod', 'pole' or 'perch' of about 16 feet (4.8 metres) was used, at the Abbey of St Denis in France, a module of 5 (or 10) 'Royal' or 'Parisian' feet of 13 inches each, and at Milan Cathedral, Spain, a module of 8 *braccia*, or arms-lengths, of about 2 feet. A module of from 5-7 feet (1.5-2.1 m) seemed to be used on Cistercian buildings.

He re-draws his scale designs life-size on the tracing shop's plaster floor. He recalls with gratitude his father's training, those years tracing scale drawings, making templates from them, then going back to brush the surface clear and start another drawing. Here is the true source of his cathedral, its curves and arches and vaults, its repeated shapes and its decorative graces.

He meets many craftsmen, with a view to employing them. He decides on a master-carpenter, and a master-smith. He interviews several stonemasons, employing most of them, but at different rates of pay depending on their skill.

Building starts

The work is under way. With templates, masons can work to the right shapes and sizes. Precision is essential: raising a massive stone to the top of the wall and finding it doesn't quite fit wastes time and money. The walls and their scaffolding are rising fast.

Down below, the stones are wheeled from carts into the lodge, shaped and carved there, ready to be positioned. All day long weighty stones are swung high in the air by cranes with grappling hooks, 'claws' lifted by worker-powered treadmills and wound up by windlasses. Carpenters have learned to build lifting gear to handle very heavy stones, doing away with the need for a great deal of scaffolding. The master's young

son comes with him sometimes and watches it all with fascination. At home he loves drawing too, like his father at the same age.

The master watches everything with satisfaction. He knows that if he is able to work here for a few years, he will see a cathedral begin to rise over the city, enough to show the bishop and Chapter that appointing him was the right decision; and to tell the city that a beautiful cathedral will be theirs in time. To accomplish his dream he works from dawn to dusk; his wife hardly sees him, she says.

A view inside Chartres Cathedral, France, shows the famous labyrinth (maze) on the floor of the nave.

Words of caution

❖ *An honourable work glorifies its master, if it stands up.* ❖
These wise words of caution were written by Lorenze Lechler, a German master-mason, in his 'Instructions', a booklet on design that he put together for his son in 1516.

FULFILMENT
AND RETIREMENT

The master works for ten years on the cathedral, until it has risen high into the air, almost to its roofline, higher than he had expected to see it. It is many years from completion, but still a magnificent sight visible from miles away on the roads into the city.

He is now 50, and beginning to wish that he had the energy he once had and that he envies – proudly – in his son, an accomplished stone-carver already. A younger man would find it easier to spend the day endlessly climbing stairs and ladders to check on the progress of the work.

Leaving the cathedral

It is the right time to leave, for the cathedral and for him. His work over the last 20 years has made him very prosperous; he can afford now to bring his career as a stonemason to an end. One last piece of carving he wishes to do, and that is an image of himself as master-mason, contemplating the model that he showed the bishop and Chapter 11 years ago.

The bishop and Chapter agree to this last suggestion. They greatly value all he has done. One of their rewards to him is to assure him that his designs and plans will be followed by any master-mason who succeeds him. Another – jokingly – is to promise they will not order him out of retirement, whatever difficulties the cathedral may have in the future.

They also wish to have a tombstone for him in the cathedral, when eventually he dies. He knows this is a very great honour, and he accepts.

Adam Kraft, the 15th-century master-mason of St Lorenz, Nuremberg, sculpted his own self-portrait, with his mallet in hand.

Some people couldn't stop building. The 14th-century Italian merchant, Datini, had what the Italians called *la malattia del calcinaccio* – 'rubble disease'. A friend's letter is full of concern that while his house is being built he spends whole days:

❖ *... among masons, workmen, mortar, sand, stones, cries and despair... No cart is filled without your lending a hand, no stone or brick laid without your changing its place, with a lot of shouting and general carry-on.* ❖

The solid central tower of the cathedral in Wells, Somerset, soars above the surrounding countryside.

At the end of medieval times, there developed a new interest in the classical world, and in the harmony of its buildings, particularly as contrasted with 'Gothic' architecture, as the dominant medieval style began to be called. Classical architecture was refined and harmonious, 'gothic' crude and backward. Buildings began to be designed by a new kind of architect-scholar whose experience and ideas were not craft-based, not derived from working practically on building sites, but essentially from books and theories. This kind of 'architect' began to replace the master-mason. In the 1570s Philip II of Spain employed as official architect Juan de Herrera, a man with no practical experience of either building or design.

Final projects

So he leaves the cathedral. But his master-mason days are not over. He has one more project, to build a farmhouse a mile or two outside the town, where he has always kept sheep and cattle. He will live a more settled and quiet life there, amongst fields, animals and orchards. He throws himself into this final work, a mainly timber building, hiring carpenters, tilers and brick-layers, but keeping the building and design under his own control.

In a year or so, the house is almost finished and he moves in. Soon he is spending most of his time farming his small estate with his wife at his side, and the rest of it making a start there on his final, final building – a house for his son.

END OF A LIFE

Though, at the good age of 60, the mason thinks of death, he doesn't brood over it. He feels lucky to feel well. He remembers mason friends who, like his father, have died not being able to breathe, their lungs choked with stone dust. He thinks of all the men he has seen over the years, and women labourers too, who have fallen – or been pushed – from scaffolding or roofs, or been crushed by carts or toppling stones or killed by them falling from above. He has survived many years of dangerous work. And no-one – he knows of one master-mason who was a victim – has murdered him.

A memorial slab over the grave of a 17th-century stonemason. It would be a great honour for the mason to be commemorated in this way.

His achievements

He is proud of what he has achieved, especially some of his memorable carvings, which other masons now travel to admire and make sketches of, and of course the new cathedral that he regularly goes to see. Work has even begun on the spire – his spire, for true to their promise, the bishop and Chapter have kept scrupulously to his original designs.

The mason finally falls ill from one of the great waves of sickness that pass over the land every few years. He dies within days, without taking Extreme Unction – the final anointing by the priest, before death, with a final confession of sins: like many people, he believed that it would only make death more likely.

Funeral Mass

The Statutes of Regensberg, Switzerland, stipulate that if a master-builder dies while he is working on a building site:

❖ *A Mass must be said for the soul of the deceased. All the masters and workers should be present and should make a small financial contribution.* ❖

Medieval facts

When he died in 1263, Hugues Libergier, master-builder of St Nicaise in Reims, France, was accorded the great honour of a tombstone in the church. His engraved figure, as befitting a person of status, stands under an arch, wearing a hat, a long robe and a hooded cloak. He is holding a model of the church and a measuring rod. At his feet are a set-square and a pair of dividers, the other essential tools of his profession. Clearly he was a socially important figure.

Commemoration of his work

His grief-stricken wife and son, and family friends, watch over his body at the wake. Later, Mass is sung for him, attended by all the stonemasons working on the cathedral, as well as many other workers. He is buried in the cathedral itself.

The Church pays for his funeral, and arranges for a Mass to be sung every year for the master's soul. A tombstone is begun, which will have a carving of the master-mason, complete with robe, set-square and compass, to be done by his successor, the master-mason who now hopes to build much of the rest of the cathedral.

In his will, the master-mason leaves all his tools and books of drawings to his son, except for the drawings done for the cathedral, which he leaves to the cathedral lodge. He bequeathes enough money to maintain and train two apprentices there. His best work will remain for hundreds of years in the standing structure of the cathedral.

This fine statue in Dijon, France, depicts Claud Suter, the master-mason who built the ducal palace there.

GLOSSARY

Alabaster ❖ a stone especially suitable for carving statues

Almonry ❖ a place from which alms were distributed

Apprentice ❖ someone undergoing formal training for a set period – rough-mason apprenticeships might last only three years, others five or seven years

Artisan ❖ a craftsman or woman, such as an embroiderer or blacksmith

Bishop ❖ the head of a diocese – elected by the Chapter, or appointed sometimes by the Pope or the King

Buttress ❖ a mass of stone or brick built against a wall to give it strength

Capital ❖ the top of a column

Chancel ❖ the east end of a church or cathedral, with the altar

Chapter ❖ the governing body of a church or cathedral, led or presided over by the bishop

Choir ❖ the part of the chancel where the religious officials stood and sat to perform the offices

Crypt ❖ the burial place under the church or cathedral

Diocese ❖ a district under the control of a bishop

Dress ❖ to dress stone is to carve it to size

Due ❖ an amount to be paid

Endowment ❖ a gift of money, usually to a religious or educational foundation

Fabric Roll ❖ the record of costs and payments on everything from wages to the purchase of stone itself – called a 'roll' because the parchment it was written on was rolled up

Feudalism ❖ the system of holding land in return for agreed services, 'works' or payment in kind

Fine ❖ a fee or charge

Flying buttress ❖ a buttress standing separate from the wall it buttresses and 'flying' up to it

Freemason ❖ a word used in later medieval times for the mason who carved stone

Freestone ❖ stone suitable for carving

Gargoyle ❖ or gurgle-hole – a carving, sometimes grotesque, on a stone rainwater spout

Gothic ❖ a style of architecture prevalent in Europe from the 12th-16th centuries, characterised by pointed arches

Guild ❖ an organisation of members of a certain craft, with rules for working, and for the production and sale of materials; also called a 'mystery'

Imaginator ❖ a carver of images, a 'sculptor'

Impressment ❖ conscription or summons by the King or the Church to work on a building project

Lodge ❖ a simple covered wooden structure built against the wall of a building where work was done and tools kept; later on, also a body of masons working there

Lord ❖ the male tenant of a manor held from the tenant of a larger estate or manor; the 'lady of the manor' is a female with the same rights

Manor ❖ a feudal estate held by a lord, with its own manor court

Mason ❖ a worker in stone

Mass ❖ the central religious service of the medieval Church, enacting the ceremonial consumption of bread and wine, 'the body and blood of Christ'; sung by the priest in Latin

Master-mason ❖ mason in charge of all the craftsmen and workers on a site, and often the designer ('architect' in modern terms) of a building

Money ❖ 1d = 1p, 240d = 100p, 20s (shillings) = £1, 1 mark = 13s 4d [= 65p]

Nobles ❖ high-ranking people such as lords or archbishops; also a coin

Patron ❖ someone who contributed funds to start up and support building projects

Priest ❖ the clerk in charge of the church; sometimes a rector or vicar

Primer ❖ a small handwritten manuscript with extracts for children to learn to read from

Payment in kind ❖ payment with articles of produce, like eggs

Relief ❖ carving shapes onto stone so that they stand out

Rough-dress ❖ a first stage in shaping stone roughly to size

Rough-mason ❖ a mason who only roughly shaped stone, before it was handed to a carver, cutter or freemason to shape precisely

Scapple ❖ to rough-dress stone

Screen ❖ a stone or wood structure separating the nave of a church from the choir and chancel

Stone-cutter or cutter ❖ a stonemason who carved stone to precise shapes and sizes

Template ❖ a frame or piece of wood (or zinc in later times) shaped exactly to the desired size and dimensions of stones to be carved

Tracery ❖ thin ribs of stonework

Tracing-floor ❖ the area where full-scale drawings of parts of a building were incised in plaster – which could be brushed down to take later drawings

Under-mason ❖ deputy or second-in-command to the master-mason

Wake ❖ the ceremony of 'watching', overnight, the dead person's body

Windlass ❖ a wooden structure for winding up weights with pulleys

TIMELINE

Useful medieval history websites

www.fordham.edu/halsall/sbook.html

A website where you can read many original documents.

www.pitt.edu/-medart/

For images of medieval art and architecture.

www.thais.it

For images of Italian sculpture and architecture.

www.the-orb.net

The website for the On-Line Reference Book for Medieval Studies.

www.trytel.com

A website that provides much original source material.

c.910 on	feudalism established
1065	dedication of Westminster Abbey
1066	William of Normandy crowned King of England
1085	Domesday Book survey
1093	Durham Cathedral begun
1096	Norwich Cathedral begun
1096	crusades begin
1098	Cistercian Order founded
c.1100 on	powerful religious revival in the 12th and 13th centuries
1107	Winchester Cathedral tower falls
1110 on	Anglo-Norman churches with carved chevron pattern in England
1137	work starts on Abbey of St Denis, Paris
1162	Thomas Becket consecrated as Archbishop of Canterbury
1163	Cathedral of Notre Dame begun in Paris
1170	murder of Becket by knights, believing it to be what Henry wanted
1174	Henry does penance for murder of Becket
1174	fire at Canterbury Cathedral – rebuilding starts
1194	fire at Chartres Cathedral – rebuilding begins
1207	order of St Francis formed
1208	King John of England quarrels with Pope
1209	Magdeburg Cathedral begun
1214	barons demand charter of liberties from John
1215	Magna Carta
1216	St Dominic's order of friars (travelling preachers) approved by Pope
1218	rebuilding of Salisbury Cathedral in Gothic style
1220	work starts in Amiens Cathedral
1222	work starts on Burgos and Toledo cathedrals
1230	King Henry III campaigning in France
1248	work starts on Cologne Cathedral
1256	work starts on angel choir, Lincoln Cathedral
1260	design for Strasbourg Cathedral drawn up
1277	work starts on Edward I's castles in North Wales
1305	Clement V becomes Pope – moves papacy to Avignon
1337-1453	Hundred Years War between France and England
1348-1349	arrival of the Black Death in Europe
1361	plague breaks out again
1377	Avignon 'captivity' of papacy ended
1389	first translation of Bible into English
1414-18	end of Great Papal Schism
1449-71	Colonia family are master-masons at Burgos and Vallodolid cathedrals
1440	Henry VI founds Eton College
1450	invention of printing with moveable type
1450-71	Wars of the Roses
1460s	first medieval books on architecture begin to be published
1490	Edward IV's youngest daughter enters a nunnery
1530s	dissolution of monasteries and nunneries in England

INDEX

A

abbeys 9, 22-23, 24, 26, 28, 33, 36
accidents 14, 40
alabaster 26, 35, 42
almonry 9, 42
apprentices 15, 16, 17, 29, 31, 32, 41, 42
architects 25, 32, 39

B

baptism 10, 11
bishop 24, 25, 26, 27, 30, 32, 33, 34, 35, 37, 38, 40, 42
Black Death 8, 43
blacksmiths 28, 33, 36, 37, 42
bridges 18-19
buttresses, flying 28, 35, 42

C

capitals 26, 27, 42
carpenters 31, 33, 36, 37, 39
castles 9, 15, 20-21, 28, 43
cathedrals 8, 9, 12, 15, 22, 25, 26, 32-39, 40, 41, 42
    Aix-la Chapelle 33
    Burgos 16, 43
    Chartres 37, 43
    Duomo 32
    Ferrara 26
    Gloucester 35
    Laon 24, 34
    Milan 36
    Valencia 25
    Wells 39
Chapter 29, 31, 32, 33, 34, 37, 38, 40, 42
childbirth 10
church 9, 10, 11, 12, 14-17, 22-29, 30, 32, 40
Church 9, 11, 41
churching 11
colleges 9, 21, 25, 30-31
craftsmen 23, 33, 37, 39, 42
cranes 15, 28, 37

D/E/F

designs 13, 17, 18, 20, 22, 24, 25, 26, 29, 30, 32, 33, 34-35, 36, 37, 40
drawings 13, 17, 18, 22, 24, 25, 26, 28, 30, 32, 33, 34, 37, 41
education 12-13
exorcism 10, 11
feudalism 8, 42
foundations 28, 36
Freemasons 29, 42
freestone 18, 23, 42
funeral 41

G

games 12, 13
gargoyles 23, 26, 42
glaziers 33
godparents 10, 11

H/I/L

hours, working 20
Hundred Years War 8, 43
illnesses 8, 12, 13, 40
imaginator 24, 25, 32, 42
impressment 20, 21, 42
labourers 15, 16, 18, 20, 40
lime-pits 35
lodges 21, 22, 26, 28-29, 30, 31, 37, 41, 42

M

marble 26, 35
mark, stonemason's 15, 17, 18, 27
Mass 40, 41, 42
master-masons 14, 15, 16, 18, 19, 22, 23, 24, 26, 27, 29, 30, 32-39, 40, 41
measurements 36
midwife 10
monasteries 9, 27
mortar 13, 16, 28, 35, 36, 39

P/Q/R

painters 27, 33
plumbers 33
priests 10, 11, 12, 40, 42
quacks 13
quarries 13, 14-15, 19, 30, 35
relics 34
remedies 13
rough-masons 18-19, 20, 42

S

saints 10, 26, 27, 34
scaffolding 14, 16, 37, 40
sculptors 23, 25, 27, 42
sculpture 23, 25, 26, 27, 38, 40, 41
sites, building 9, 13, 14-17, 19, 21, 22, 30, 31, 34, 36, 37, 39, 40, 42
spires 28, 34, 35, 40
stone,
    rough-dressing 14, 15, 17, 18, 19, 20, 21, 22, 42
    types of 15, 26, 35
stone-carvers 17, 23, 24, 25, 26-29, 30, 32, 33, 38, 42
stone-cutters 17, 18, 22, 23, 32, 42
stonemason,
    birth 10-11
    career 18-37
    childhood 12-13
    death 40-41
    education 12-13
    retirement 38-40
    training 14-17

T

templates 17, 18, 21, 22, 37, 42
tombstones 26, 27, 38, 40, 41
tools 9, 13, 14, 15, 17, 20, 21, 22, 23, 24, 28, 29, 30, 31, 40, 41
towers 16, 25, 28, 34, 35, 39
tracing-floor 17, 30, 37, 42

U/V

under-masons 15, 20, 21, 23, 30-31, 32, 33, 42
wages 15, 18, 20, 21, 33, 37
wake 41, 42
workshops 17, 30

These are the lists of contents for each title in *Medieval Lives*:

Peasant

Introduction · First years · Peasant cottage · Childhood
The Church · Marriage · Land · Work-service for the manor · The manorial court
The working year · Feeding the family · Sickness and health · Women's work · Earning money
Games and entertainment · Freedom · Last days · Glossary · Timeline/Useful websites · Index

Merchant

Introduction · First days · House and home · Growing up · School · Becoming a merchant
Marriage · The wool trade · Travel and communication · War and piracy · Secrets of success
Branching out · Wealth and property · The merchant's wife · Good works · Health and diet
The end · Glossary · Timeline/Useful websites · Index

Knight

All about knights · A future knight is born · Time to leave home · Becoming a squire
A squire goes forth · Becoming a knight · Invitation to the castle · Joust! · Called to war
Battlefield tactics · Dressed to kill · Weapons · Siege warfare · Pilgrimage · Returning home
Knightly duties · Death of a knight · Glossary · Timeline/Useful websites · Index

Nun

Introduction · Birth · Childhood and education · To the nunnery – postulant
The nunnery itself · Taking the veil – novice · Daily life – the offices · The inner life
Daily routine · Enclosure · Cellaress and librarian · The world outside · Priests and nuns
Poverty and personal possessions · A visitation · Difficult times · Death · Glossary
Timeline/Useful websites · Index

Lady of the Manor

A medieval lady · A lady is born · Invitation to a wedding
At home with a lady · Wifely duties · Noble children · A year in the life
Clothes and hairstyles · A lady's hobbies · A lady's books · Time to eat · The lady falls ill
Women who work · The noblest ladies · A visit to a nunnery · The world outside
Widowhood · Glossary · Timeline/Useful websites · Index

Stonemason

Introduction · Birth · Childhood and growing up · Training - the quarry
Training - the building site · Rough-mason – a bridge · Summoned to work - a castle
A real 'mason' - the abbey · A growing reputation · Stone-carver · The lodge
Under-mason for the college · Master-mason for the cathedral · Designing the cathedral
Building the cathedral · Retirement · End of a life · Glossary · Timeline/Useful websites · Index